Dr. Martin L.

SUBTRACTION
and
ADDITION

MATH BUSTERS

Rebecca Wingard-Nelson

NEED MORE PRACTICE?
Free worksheets available at
http://www.enslow.com

E | **Enslow Publishers, Inc.**
40 Industrial Road
Box 398
Berkeley Heights, NJ 07922
USA
http://www.enslow.com

Library of Congress Cataloging-in-Publication Data

Wingard-Nelson, Rebecca.
Subtraction and addition / Rebecca Wingard-Nelson.
      p. cm. — (Math busters series)
    Includes bibliographical references and index.
    ISBN-13: 978-0-7660-2875-3
    ISBN-10: 0-7660-2875-5
  1. Subtraction—Juvenile literature. 2. Addition—Juvenile literature. I. Title.
    QA115.W7545 2008
  513.2'11—dc22

                                                  2006037085

10 9 8 7 6 5 4 3 2 1

To Our Readers: We have done our best to make sure all Internet Addresses in this book were active and appropriate when we went to press. However, the author and the publisher have no control over and assume no liability for the material available on those Internet sites or on other Web sites they may link to. Any comments or suggestions can be sent by e-mail to comments@enslow.com or to the address on the back cover.

Illustration credits: © Birch Design Studios/Artzooks, pp. 9, 11, 17, 21, 25, 27, 29, 35, 37, 38, 40, 43, 47, 58; © 2007 Jupiterimages Corporation, pp. 52, 56, 60

Cover photo: © 2007 Jupiterimages Corporation

Free Worksheets are available for this book at http://www.enslow.com. Search on the **Math Busters** series name. The publisher will provide access to the worksheets for five years from the book's first publication date.

Contents

Introduction

Not every person is an accountant,
engineer, rocket scientist, or math teacher.
However, every person does use math.

Most people never think, "I just used math to decide if I have
enough milk for this week!" But that is exactly what they did.
Math is everywhere; we just don't see it because it doesn't
always look like the math we do at school.

Math gives you the power to
• determine the best route on a trip
• keep score in a game
• choose the better buy
• figure a sale price
• plan a vacation schedule

Addition and subtraction are the most basic math operations.
They are used in every person's daily life.
Addition tells you how much you are spending
when you buy more than one thing.
Subtraction helps you compare sizes, prices, and amounts.

This book will help you understand
subtraction and addition.
It can be read from beginning to end,
or used to review a specific topic.

① Adding **Whole** Numbers

You can add numbers together
to find how many you have in all.

Counting On

Marlon has 3 guppies. Jeri gives him 2 more. How many guppies does Marlon have in all?

One way to add is to count on.

Step 1: Marlon starts with 3 guppies. 3

Step 2: Jeri gives him 2 more.
Begin with 3, count on 2 more.

$$3 \quad 4 \quad 5$$
$$1 \qquad 2$$

$$3 + 2 = 5$$

Write answers using sentences like this . . .

Marlon has 5 guppies in all.

or units like this.

5 guppies

Addition Terms

Numbers that are added are called **addends.**   **3 + 2** = 5

Answers to addition problems are called **sums.**   3 + 2 = **5**

Addition problems may be written in a line or a column.

$$3 + 2 = 5$$

$$\begin{array}{r} 3 \\ + 2 \\ \hline 5 \end{array}$$

Learn the Facts

The one-digit numbers are 0, 1, 2, 3, 4, 5, 6, 7, 8, and 9. This table shows the one-digit addition facts that have one-digit answers.

1 + 0 = 1 1 + 5 = 6 1 + 1 = 2 1 + 6 = 7 1 + 2 = 3 1 + 7 = 8 1 + 3 = 4 1 + 8 = 9 1 + 4 = 5	4 + 0 = 4 4 + 1 = 5 4 + 2 = 6 4 + 3 = 7 4 + 4 = 8 4 + 5 = 9	7 + 0 = 7 7 + 1 = 8 7 + 2 = 9	
2 + 0 = 2 2 + 4 = 6 2 + 1 = 3 2 + 5 = 7 2 + 2 = 4 2 + 6 = 8 2 + 3 = 5 2 + 7 = 9	5 + 0 = 5 5 + 1 = 6 5 + 2 = 7 5 + 3 = 8 5 + 4 = 9	8 + 0 = 8 8 + 1 = 9	
3 + 0 = 3 3 + 4 = 7 3 + 1 = 4 3 + 5 = 8 3 + 2 = 5 3 + 6 = 9 3 + 3 = 6	6 + 0 = 6 6 + 1 = 7 6 + 2 = 8 6 + 3 = 9	9 + 0 = 9	

Use the Facts

Trina has 6 wristbands. She buys 3 more.
How many wristbands does Trina have in all?

To solve this problem, add 6 + 3.

Step 1: Use basic addition facts to find the sum.   6 + 3 = 9

Trina has
9 wristbands in all.

Addition gives you the
POWER
to understand other math operations.
Subtraction is the opposite of addition.
Multiplication is repeated addition.

② Regrouping Power: Addition

Sometimes when you add
a one-digit number, the sum has two digits.
Use place value to regroup.

Place Value

Place value tells you how much each digit in a number stands for.

62 is the same as			**457 is the same as**		
6	2		4	5	7
6 tens	2 ones		4 hundreds	5 tens	7 ones

Regrouping Ones

What is 7 + 5?

Step 1: Put dots under each number in the problem.
Make a box with ten sections.

7 + 5

Step 2: Move 7 dots into the box.

7 + 5

Step 3: Use some of the 5 dots to fill the box. There are 2 dots left outside the box.
You have 1 group of ten in the box, and 2 ones left outside.

7 + 5

1 2
ten ones

Another way to say **1 ten and 2 ones** is **12**.

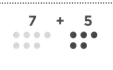 7 + 5 = 12

Learn the Facts

This table shows the one-digit addition facts with two-digit sums.

1 + 9 = 10	4 + 6 = 10 4 + 7 = 11 4 + 8 = 12 4 + 9 = 13	7 + 3 = 10 7 + 4 = 11 7 + 5 = 12 7 + 6 = 13	7 + 7 = 14 7 + 8 = 15 7 + 9 = 16
2 + 8 = 10 2 + 9 = 11	5 + 5 = 10 5 + 6 = 11 5 + 7 = 12 5 + 8 = 13 5 + 9 = 14	8 + 2 = 10 8 + 3 = 11 8 + 4 = 12 8 + 5 = 13	8 + 6 = 14 8 + 7 = 15 8 + 8 = 16 8 + 9 = 17
3 + 7 = 10 3 + 8 = 11 3 + 9 = 12	6 + 4 = 10 6 + 5 = 11 6 + 6 = 12 6 + 7 = 13 6 + 8 = 14 6 + 9 = 15	9 + 1 = 10 9 + 2 = 11 9 + 3 = 12 9 + 4 = 13 9 + 5 = 14	9 + 6 = 15 9 + 7 = 16 9 + 8 = 17 9 + 9 = 18

Use the Facts

Mark made 9 drawings of buildings and 4 drawings of gardens. How many drawings did Mark make in all?

To solve this problem, add 9 + 4.

Step 1: Use addition facts to find the sum.

9 + 4 = 13

Mark made 13 drawings in all.

③ Adding Larger Numbers

Adding numbers that have more than one digit is easy when you understand place value.

Place Value

Before you add numbers, line up the digits in columns by their place value.

	hundreds	tens	ones
25		2	5
234	2	3	4

Adding with Place Value

Renee worked 24 days. Then she worked 11 more. How many days did Renee work?

To solve this problem, add 24 + 11.

Step 1: Column addition keeps the place values in line. Write the problem in a column. Line up the digits that have the same place value.

$$\begin{array}{r} 24 \\ +\ 11 \end{array}$$

Step 2: Add ones. 4 + 1 = 5. Write a 5 in the ones place.

$$\begin{array}{r} 24 \\ +\ 11 \\ \hline 5 \end{array}$$

Step 3: Add tens. 2 + 1 = 3. Write a 3 in the tens place.

$$\begin{array}{r} 24 \\ +\ 11 \\ \hline 35 \end{array}$$

Renee worked 35 days in all.

Larger Numbers

Mr. Snethen has a big glass case in his classroom with 1,224 bugs in it. He also has a display in the hallway with 352 bugs in it. How many bugs does Mr. Snethen have in all?

To solve this problem, add 1,224 + 352.

Step 1: Write the problem in a column. Line up digits with the same place value.

```
  1224
+  352
  1576
```

Step 2: All numbers with more than one digit are added one place value at a time. Add ones. 4 + 2 = 6. Write a 6 in the ones place.

```
  1224
+  352
     6
```

Step 3: Add tens. 2 + 5 = 7. Write a 7 in the tens place.

```
  1224
+  352
    76
```

Step 4: Add hundreds. 2 + 3 = 5. Write a 5 in the hundreds place.

```
  1224
+  352
   576
```

Step 5: Add thousands. When there is no digit in a place, treat it as a zero. 1 + 0 = 1. Write a 1 in the thousands place.

```
  1224
+  352
  1576
```

Mr. Snethen has 1,576 bugs in all.

FACT BUSTER!

One-digit addition facts give you the power to solve any addition problem.

Memorizing the facts is the key.

Multi-Digit Regrouping: Addition

Added numbers may be
regrouped in any place value.
Regrouping can occur in more than one place.

Addition with Regrouping

Bryant needs 67 red bricks and 28 brown bricks for his patio. How many bricks does Bryant need in all?

To solve this problem, add 67 + 28.

Step 1: Write the problem in a column. Line up digits with the same place value.	67 + 28

Step 2: Add ones. 7 + 8 = 15. 15 ones is the same as 1 ten and 5 ones. Write a 5 in the ones place. Carry a 1 to the tens place.	1 67 + 28 5

Step 3: Add tens. Remember to add the 1 you carried from the ones place. 1 + 6 + 2 = 9. Write a 9 in the tens place.	1 67 + 28 95

Bryant needs 95 bricks in all.

Regrouping names the same values in different ways.

16 can be thought of as 16 ones, or as 1 ten and 6 ones.

Addition Regrouping

Regrouping in addition combines a group of small units into a larger unit.

10 ones is the same as 1 ten (10).

10 tens is the same as 1 hundred (100).

10 hundreds is the same as 1 thousand (1,000).

10 thousands is the same as 1 ten-thousand (10,000).

10 ten-thousands is the same as 1 hundred-thousand (100,000).

10 hundred-thousands is the same a 1 million (1,000,000).

Regrouping More than Once

Add 2,462 + 857

Step 1: Write the problem in a column. Line up digits with the same place value.

```
  2462
+  857
```

Step 2: Add ones. 2 + 7 = 9. Write a 9 in the ones place.

```
  2462
+  857
     9
```

Step 3: Add tens. 6 + 5 = 11. 11 tens is the same as 1 hundred and 1 ten. Write a 1 in the tens place. Carry a 1 to the hundreds place.

```
 1
  2462
+  857
    19
```

Step 4: Add hundreds. Remember to add the 1 you carried from the tens place. 1 + 4 + 8 = 13. Write a 3 in the hundreds place. Carry a 1 to the thousands place.

```
 11
  2462
+  857
   319
```

Step 5: Add thousands. 1 + 2 + 0 = 3. Write a 3 in the thousands place.

```
 11
  2462
+  857
  3319
```

2,462 + 857 = 3,319

A property is a trait
that a thing always has.
A property of sugar is sweetness.
Addition has some important properties.

The Commutative Property

When you add two numbers, changing the order of the numbers does not change the sum.

Test It

Is 14 + 23 the same as 23 + 14?

Add 14 + 23, then add 23 + 14.

Step 1: Add 14 + 23.
14 + 23 = 37.

$$\begin{array}{r} 14 \\ + 23 \\ \hline 37 \end{array}$$

Step 2: Add 23 + 14.
23 + 14 = 37.

$$\begin{array}{r} 23 \\ + 14 \\ \hline 37 \end{array}$$

The sums are the same.

The commutative property makes learning facts easier. When you know one fact, change the order of the numbers, and you know another one!
3 + 2 = 5   2 + 3 = 5

The Associative Property

When you add more than two numbers, it does not matter which numbers you add first. The sum will be the same.

Test It

Is (6 + 2) + 3 the same as 6 + (2 + 3)?

Parentheses tell you what numbers to add first.

Step 1: Add (6 + 2) + 3.
Add 6 + 2 first. Then add 3 more.
8 + 3 = 11

$$
\begin{array}{r}
(6 + 2) + 3 \\
8 \quad + 3 \\
11
\end{array}
$$

Step 2: Add 6 + (2 + 3).
Add 2 + 3 first. Then add 6 more.
6 + 5 = 11

$$
\begin{array}{r}
6 + (2 + 3) \\
6 + \quad 5 \\
11
\end{array}
$$

The sums are the same.

The Zero Property

When you add zero and any number, the answer is that number.

Test It

Add 6 + 0.

6 + 0 = 6

Add 0 + 854.

0 + 854 = 854

The value of a number does not change when zero is added.

⑥ Subtracting Whole Numbers

Just like with addition facts,
once you know the basic subtraction facts,
subtracting any numbers is easy.

Subtraction

Anna has 7 red and blue pens. She separated the pens by color.
There are 2 red pens. How many blue pens are there?

To solve this problem, subtract 7 – 2.

Step 1: Begin with 7.

○ ○ ○ ○
○ ○ ○

Step 2: Move 2 away. These 2 are
the red pens.

●   ○ ○ ○
●   ○ ○

Step 3: The pens that are left are blue.

●   ● ● ●
●   ● ●

7 – 2 = 5
There are 5 blue pens.

Subtraction Terms

Some of the subtraction terms you may hear are listed below.

minuend—The number from which you subtract.	7
subtrahend—The number you subtract.	– 2
difference—The answer to a subtraction problem.	5

minuend - subtrahend = difference
    7   -   2   =   5

Learn the Facts

This table shows the subtraction facts.

0 - 0 = 0	1 - 1 = 0	2 - 2 = 0	3 - 3 = 0	4 - 4 = 0
1 - 0 = 1	2 - 1 = 1	3 - 2 = 1	4 - 3 = 1	5 - 4 = 1
2 - 0 = 2	3 - 1 = 2	4 - 2 = 2	5 - 3 = 2	6 - 4 = 2
3 - 0 = 3	4 - 1 = 3	5 - 2 = 3	6 - 3 = 3	7 - 4 = 3
4 - 0 = 4	5 - 1 = 4	6 - 2 = 4	7 - 3 = 4	8 - 4 = 4
5 - 0 = 5	6 - 1 = 5	7 - 2 = 5	8 - 3 = 5	9 - 4 = 5
6 - 0 = 6	7 - 1 = 6	8 - 2 = 6	9 - 3 = 6	10 - 4 = 6
7 - 0 = 7	8 - 1 = 7	9 - 2 = 7	10 - 3 = 7	11 - 4 = 7
8 - 0 = 8	9 - 1 = 8	10 - 2 = 8	11 - 3 = 8	12 - 4 = 8
9 - 0 = 9	10 - 1 = 9	11 - 2 = 9	12 - 3 = 9	13 - 4 = 9
5 - 5 = 0	6 - 6 = 0	7 - 7 = 0	8 - 8 = 0	9 - 9 = 0
6 - 5 = 1	7 - 6 = 1	8 - 7 = 1	9 - 8 = 1	10 - 9 = 1
7 - 5 = 2	8 - 6 = 2	9 - 7 = 2	10 - 8 = 2	11 - 9 = 2
8 - 5 = 3	9 - 6 = 3	10 - 7 = 3	11 - 8 = 3	12 - 9 = 3
9 - 5 = 4	10 - 6 = 4	11 - 7 = 4	12 - 8 = 4	13 - 9 = 4
10 - 5 = 5	11 - 6 = 5	12 - 7 = 5	13 - 8 = 5	14 - 9 = 5
11 - 5 = 6	12 - 6 = 6	13 - 7 = 6	14 - 8 = 6	15 - 9 = 6
12 - 5 = 7	13 - 6 = 7	14 - 7 = 7	15 - 8 = 7	16 - 9 = 7
13 - 5 = 8	14 - 6 = 8	15 - 7 = 8	16 - 8 = 8	17 - 9 = 8
14 - 5 = 9	15 - 6 = 9	16 - 7 = 9	17 - 8 = 9	18 - 9 = 9

Use the Facts

Mikal went on a 7-day cruise. On 5 of the days it rained. How many days were without rain?

To solve this problem, subtract 7 - 5.

Step 1: Use basic subtraction facts to find the difference.

7 - 5 = 2

There were 2 days without rain.

Subtraction is the
opposite, or inverse, of addition.
Addition is the inverse of subtraction.
Inverse operations do the opposite of each other.
Addition puts together, subtraction takes apart.

Fact Families

For every addition fact, there is a related subtraction fact. When you know 3 + 4 = 7, then you also know 7 – 4 = 3. You add 4 in the addition fact; you take away 4 in the subtraction fact.

3 + 4 = 7   7 – 4 = 3

The commutative property (see page 14) tells you that when you know 3 + 4 = 7, then you know 4 + 3 = 7. The related subtraction fact for 4 + 3 = 7 is 7 – 3 = 4.

4 + 3 = 7   7 – 3 = 4

The four related facts   3 + 4 = 7   7 – 4 = 3
are called a fact family.   4 + 3 = 7   7 – 3 = 4

What are the related facts for 8 + 9 = 17?

Step 1: Use the commutative property to find the related addition fact.	8 + 9 = 17 9 + 8 = 17
Step 2: Find the related subtraction facts.	17 – 9 = 8 17 – 8 = 9

Addition checks subtraction.
Subtraction checks addition.

Why Subtract?

There is more than one reason to subtract.

- **To compare, or find the difference in, amounts.**

    Ben has 6 books, Jill has 2. Subtract to find how
    many more books Ben has than Jill. 6 – 2 = 4

- **To take one amount from another.**

    You have $4 and spend $3. Subtract to find
    how much you have left. $4 – $3 = $1

- **To find part of a quantity when you know the total
  and the other part.**

    There are 16 math problems. So far, 9 have been solved.
    Subtract to find how many are left to solve. 16 – 9 = 7

- **To check the answer to an addition problem.**

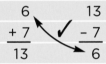

$$
\begin{array}{cc}
6 & 13 \\
+\,7 & -\,7 \\
\hline
13 & 6
\end{array}
$$

Check the Difference

*You just solved the subtraction problem 26 – 19 = 7.
Check to see that your answer is right.*

Step 1: Use addition to check that
subtraction answers are right.
Add the answer (7) to the number
you subtracted (19).

$$26 – 19 = 7$$

$$
\begin{array}{r}
19 \\
+\ 7 \\
\hline
26
\end{array}
$$

**The sum (26) is the same number you started with,
so the answer is right.**

⑧ Subtracting Larger Numbers

Most whole numbers
have more than one digit.
Use place value to subtract these numbers.

Subtraction with Place Value

Subtract 64 – 23.

Step 1: Write the problem in a column
to keep place values in order.
Line up digits with the same place value.

$$\begin{array}{r} 64 \\ -\ 23 \\ \hline \end{array}$$

Step 2: Subtract from right to left,
beginning in the ones place.
Subtract ones.

$$\begin{array}{r} 64 \\ -\ 23 \\ \hline 1 \end{array}$$

Step 3: Subtract tens.

64 – 23 = 41

$$\begin{array}{r} 64 \\ -\ 23 \\ \hline 41 \end{array}$$

You can add and subtract
numbers of any size.
Just do one place at a time.

Always add and subtract
from right to left.

Subtracting Larger Numbers

Subtract 2,567 – 1,543.

Step 1: Write the problem in a column.
Line up digits with the same place value.

```
  2567
- 1543
```

Step 2: Subtract from right to left,
beginning in the ones place.
Subtract ones.

```
  2567
- 1543
     4
```

Step 3: Subtract tens.

```
  2567
- 1543
    24
```

Step 4: Subtract hundreds.

```
  2567
- 1543
   024
```

Step 5: Subtract thousands.

2,567 – 1,543 = 1024

```
  2567
- 1543
  1024
```

*Gus drove to his cousin's house.
They live 227 miles apart, but
Gus got lost and drove 268 miles.
How many extra miles did
Gus drive?*

To solve this problem,
subtract 268 – 227.

Step 1: Write the problem in a column.
Subtract ones.

```
  268
- 227
    1
```

Step 2: Subtract tens.

```
  268
- 227
   41
```

Step 3: Subtract hundreds.

Gus drove 41 extra miles.

```
  268
- 227
   41
```

Sometimes the digit you are subtracting is greater than the digit from which you are subtracting.

Subtraction with Regrouping

Subtract 23 – 6.

Step 1: Write the problem in a column. Line up digits with the same place value.

$$\begin{array}{r} 23 \\ -\ 6 \\ \hline \end{array}$$

Step 2: Look at the ones column. You can not subtract because 6 ones are greater than 3 ones. Regroup.

$$\begin{array}{r} 23 \\ -\ 6 \\ \hline \end{array}$$

2 tens and 3 ones is the same as 1 ten and 13 ones.

Write the regrouped values above each column. Cross out the original digits to remind yourself that they have been regrouped.

$$\begin{array}{r} 1\ \ 13 \\ \not{2}\not{3} \\ -\ \ 6 \\ \hline \end{array}$$

Step 3: Subtract ones. 13 – 6 = 7

$$\begin{array}{r} 1\ \ 13 \\ \not{2}\not{3} \\ -\ \ 6 \\ \hline 7 \end{array}$$

Step 4: Subtract tens. 1 – 0 = 1

$$\begin{array}{r} 1\ \ 13 \\ \not{2}\not{3} \\ -\ \ 6 \\ \hline 17 \end{array}$$

23 – 6 = 17

Subtraction Regrouping

Regrouping in subtraction separates one large unit into a group of smaller units (1 ten becomes 10 ones).

1 ten is the same as 10 ones.

1 hundred is the same as 10 tens.

1 thousand is the same as 10 hundreds.

1 ten-thousand is the same as 10 thousands.

1 hundred-thousand is the same as 10 ten-thousands.

1 million is the same as 10 hundred-thousands.

More Regrouping

Subtract 87 – 19.

Step 1: Write the problem in a column.
Line up digits with the same place value.

$$
\begin{array}{r}
87 \\
- \ 19 \\
\end{array}
$$

Step 2: To subtract ones, you must regroup.
Regroup 1 ten as 10 ones.
8 tens and 7 ones is the same as 7 tens and 17 ones.

$$
\begin{array}{r}
7 \ 17 \\
8\!\!\!/7 \\
- \ 19 \\
\end{array}
$$

Step 3: Subtract ones. 17 – 9 = 8

$$
\begin{array}{r}
7 \ 17 \\
8\!\!\!/7 \\
- \ 19 \\
\hline
8 \\
\end{array}
$$

Step 4: Subtract tens. 7 – 1 = 6

$$
\begin{array}{r}
7 \ 17 \\
8\!\!\!/7 \\
- \ 19 \\
\hline
68 \\
\end{array}
$$

87 – 19 = 68

Regrouping in subtraction is sometimes called borrowing because you borrow from one place to give to another.

Multi-Digit Regrouping: Subtraction

For some problems,
you may need to regroup for
more than one place value.

Regrouping with Three Digits

Subtract 924 – 687.

Step 1: Write the problem in a column. Line up digits with the same place value.	924 − 687

Step 2: To subtract ones, you must regroup. Regroup 1 ten as 10 ones. 2 tens and 4 ones is the same as 1 ten and 14 ones.	1 14 92̶4̶ − 687 ‾‾‾‾ 7

Step 3: Subtract ones. 14 − 7 = 7	1 14 92̶4̶ − 687 ‾‾‾‾ 7

Step 4: To subtract tens, you must regroup. Regroup 1 hundred as 10 tens. 9 hundreds and 1 ten is the same as 8 hundreds and 11 tens.	11 8 1̶14 9̶2̶4̶ − 687 ‾‾‾‾ 7

Step 5: Subtract tens. 11 − 8 = 3	11 8 1̶14 9̶2̶4̶ − 687 ‾‾‾‾ 37

Step 6: Subtract hundreds. 8 − 6 = 2 924 − 687 = 237	11 8 1̶14 9̶2̶4̶ − 687 ‾‾‾‾ 237

24

Regrouping with Zeros

Chef Pierre created enough soup for 1,000 servings. During the day, 824 orders of soup were served. How many servings were left at the end of the day?

To solve this problem, subtract 1,000 – 824.

Step 1: Write the problem in a column. Line up digits with the same place value. When the minuend (1,000) has zeros in it, you may need to regroup in more than one place before you begin to subtract.

$$\begin{array}{r} 1000 \\ -\ 824 \end{array}$$

Step 2: To subtract ones, you must regroup. There are no tens or hundreds to regroup. Regroup 1 thousand as 10 hundreds.

$$\begin{array}{r} {}^{10} \\ \cancel{1}000 \\ -\ 824 \end{array}$$

Step 3: Regroup 10 hundreds as 9 hundreds and 10 tens.

$$\begin{array}{r} 9 \\ \cancel{10}\,10 \\ \cancel{1}\cancel{0}00 \\ -\ 824 \end{array}$$

Step 4: Regroup 10 tens as 9 tens and 10 ones.

$$\begin{array}{r} 9\ 9 \\ \cancel{10}\cancel{10}\,10 \\ \cancel{1}\cancel{0}\cancel{0}\cancel{0} \\ -\ 824 \\ \hline 176 \end{array}$$

Step 5: Subtract right to left.
10 – 4 = 6
9 – 2 = 7
9 – 8 = 1

$$\begin{array}{r} 9\ 9 \\ \cancel{10}\cancel{10}\,10 \\ \cancel{1}\cancel{0}\cancel{0}\cancel{0} \\ -\ 824 \\ \hline 176 \end{array}$$

There were 176 servings of soup left at the end of the day.

25

Mental Math Power: Addition

You can use mental math
when the numbers are easy. Sometimes
you have to use mental math because you don't
have a paper and pencil or a calculator.

Adding 9

Add 15 + 9.

It is easy to add 10 to a number. Think of 9 as 1 less than 10.
Add 10 in place of 9, then take 1 away from the sum.

Step 1: Think:	15 + 10 = 25
Step 2: Think:	1 less than 25 is 24, so 15 + 9 = 24

Grouping Tens

Add 9 + 4 + 6 + 1 + 3.

You can add these in your head by
grouping the numbers into tens.

Step 1: Find two numbers that add up to 10.	**9** + 4 + 6 + **1** + 3 9 + 1 = 10
Step 2: Find two more numbers that add up to 10. Now you have 2 groups of 10, or 20.	9 + **4** + **6** + 1 + 3 9 + 1 = 10 4 + 6 = 10
Step 3: There is a 3 left.	9 + 4 + 6 + 1 + **3** 3 ones are left 10 + 10 + 3 = 23

9 + 4 + 6 + 1 + 3 = 23

*Practicing mental math
is a brain-power workout!*

Give and Take

This weekend Dr. Morris saw 208 patients in the emergency room. Dr. Young saw 111. How many patients did they see in all?

You can take from one number and give the same amount to the other number to add these in your head.

Step 1: Think: **I need to find the sum of 208 + 111. 200 is easier to add than 208, so I'll take 8 off of 208.**

Step 2: Think: **I took 8 off 208, so I need to give 8 to 111. 111 + 8 is easy, because there is no regrouping. 111 + 8 = 119**

Step 3: Think: **Now it is easy to add. 200 + 119 = 319**

                        200 + 119 is the same as 208 + 111. Both sums are 319.

The doctors saw 319 patients in all.

⑫ Mental Math Power: Subtraction

How much money will be
left after buying that ring? How many
miles are left to drive? How many minutes are left
in the class? You can use mental subtraction to
answer these kinds of questions.

Subtracting 9

Subtract 37 – 9.

It is easy to subtract 10 from a number. Think of subtracting 9 as taking away 10, then adding 1 back.

Step 1: Think:	37 – 10 = 27
Step 2: Think:	"I subtracted 10, so I need to add 1 back to the answer."
So, 37 – 9 = 28.	27 + 1 = 28

Counting Up

Subtract 140 – 75.

Sometimes it is easier to count up from the number you are subtracting to the number you started with.

Step 1: Think:	**If I start at 75, it takes 25 more to get to 100.**
Step 2: Think:	**From 100 to 140 is 40 more.**
Step 3: Think:	**40 + 25 = 65 The difference is 65.**
So, 140 – 75 = 65.	

Easier Numbers

Look at this pattern.

18 − 9 = 9   19 − 10 = 9   23 − 18 = 5   25 − 20 = 5

You can add the same amount to the number you begin with and the number you are subtracting without changing the answer.

Charles is planning to drive 650 miles in one day. So far, he has driven 497 miles. How many miles does he have left to drive?

Step 1: Think:	If I add 3 to 497, it becomes 500, which is easy to subtract.
Step 2: Think:	If I add 3 to 497, I need to add 3 to 650. 650 + 3 = 653. The new problem is 653 − 500.
Step 3: Think:	Now it is easy to subtract. 653 − 500 = 153

Charles has 153 miles left to drive.

Mental Math Busting Tip:
Try breaking the number you are subtracting into parts. If you need to subtract 42, first subtract 40, then subtract 2 more.

Do you have enough money to
buy a shirt and book? How many yards
of fabric should you buy to make curtains?
About how far did you drive today?

Rounding

Rounding finds the closest number that ends in zero.

To round a number:	122
1. **Decide the place you are rounding to.**	Round to tens. 122
2. **Look one place to the right.**	Look at ones. 122
3. **If the digit is 5 or greater, round up.**	2 is less than 5.
If the digit is less than 5, round down.	Round down to **120**.

Rounding

Clarence drove 92 miles, then stopped for lunch. He drove another 264 miles after lunch. About how many miles did Clarence drive?

To solve this problem, estimate the sum of 264 + 92.

Step 1: Round each number before you add. If the addends have the same number of digits, round to the greatest place value. If the addends have a different number of digits, round to the greatest place value of the smaller number.

92 has fewer digits than 264. The greatest place value of 92 is the tens place. Round each number to the tens place.

264 rounds to 260.
92 rounds to 90.

Step 2: Add the rounded numbers.

$$\begin{array}{r} 260 \\ +\ 90 \\ \hline 350 \end{array}$$

Clarence drove about 350 miles.

Adjusting

Estimate 24,657 + 44,225.

Step 1: Estimate by adding only the front digits.	$\begin{array}{r} \mathbf{2}4{,}657 \\ + \mathbf{4}4{,}225 \\ \hline \end{array}$	$\begin{array}{r} \mathbf{2}0{,}000 \\ + \mathbf{4}0{,}000 \\ \hline \mathbf{6}0{,}000 \end{array}$
Step 2: Add just the digits in the next smaller place value.	$\begin{array}{r} 2\mathbf{4}{,}657 \\ + 4\mathbf{4}{,}225 \\ \hline \end{array}$	$\begin{array}{r} \mathbf{4}{,}000 \\ + \mathbf{4}{,}000 \\ \hline \mathbf{8}{,}000 \end{array}$

Step 3 : Adjust your original estimate.

8,000 is about another 10,000. Adjust the first estimate by adding another 10,000.
60,000 + 10,000 = 70,000

The estimated sum of 24,657 + 44,225 is 70,000.

The actual sum is 68,882, so 70,000 is a good estimate!

Why estimate?

To find an approximate answer. Sometimes you will not need an exact answer.

To predict. How much is it going to cost to remodel a bathroom? How many 7th-graders will there be next year?

To check an answer. To see whether your answer to a problem is reasonable.

⑭ Estimation Power: Subtraction

The same estimation skills that are used in addition are used in subtraction.

Rounding

A. *Estimate 687 – 136 by rounding to the hundreds place.*

Step 1: Round to the hundreds place.	687 rounds to 700. 136 rounds to 100.
Step 2: Subtract the rounded numbers.	700 – 100 = 600

687 – 136 is about 600.

B. *Estimate 687 – 136 by rounding to the tens place.*

Step 1: Round to the tens place.	687 rounds to 690. 136 rounds to 140.
Step 2: Subtract the rounded numbers.	690 – 140 = 550

687 – 136 is about 550.

C. *Subtract 687 – 136.*

Step 1: Line up the digits by place value.

$$\begin{array}{r} 687 \\ -\ 136 \\ \hline \end{array}$$

Step 2: Subtract.

$$\begin{array}{r} 687 \\ -\ 136 \\ \hline 551 \end{array}$$

687 – 136 = 551

When you round numbers closer to the original numbers, your estimated answer is closer to the exact answer.

Compare the estimated answers for rounding to the hundreds place (600) and rounding to the tens place (550) to the exact answer (551).

Rounding to tens gives a closer estimate than rounding to hundreds.

Over or Under?

overestimate—To estimate above the exact value.

underestimate—To estimate below the exact value.

Compatible Numbers

Giana and Miguel are putting a border around a display for the science fair. The border is sold in 126-inch rolls. They need 74 inches of border. About how many inches of border will be left if they buy one roll?

Since you only need to know about how many inches will be left, you can estimate. You can estimate by choosing numbers that are close to the original problem and that work well together.

Estimate 126 – 74 to find about how many inches will be left.

Step 1: 126 is close to 125.   126 – 74
74 is close to 75.   125 – 75
125 and 75 work well together.

Step 2: Subtract the compatible numbers.   125 – 75 = 50

**There will be about 50 inches
of border left if they buy one roll.**

Compatible numbers
are numbers that are easy
for you to add and subtract.

Compatible numbers can be
different for different
people.

Word Problem Power: Addition

You solve problems every day,
and you don't really think about it.
Math word problems are like everyday problems.
You just need a plan.

Problem-Solving Power

Word problems can be solved using 4 steps.

Step 1. Read the problem for understanding. What do you know and what are you trying to find?

Step 2. Make a plan. Can you write an equation, draw a picture, or find a pattern? There are many strategies you can try.

Step 3. Follow the plan. Use the plan you made to solve.

Step 4. Check the answer. Does the answer make sense? Double check your math.

Addition Word Problem

The students in three eighth-grade classes received free admission to a theme park as a reward for good conduct. There were 26 students in one class, 31 in another, and 28 in the third. How many students in all received free admission?

Step 1: Read the problem. What do you know? **The students in 3 classes each received free admission to a theme park.** What are you trying to find? **The number of students in all that received free admission.**

Step 2: Make a plan. The words "in all" tell you that you should add. **Add the number of students in each class to find how many received free admission.**

Step 3: Follow the plan. Write the number of students in each class in a column. Add each place from right to left. Regroup when needed.

$$\begin{array}{r} 1 \\ 26 \text{ students} \\ 31 \text{ students} \\ +\ 28 \text{ students} \\ \hline 85 \text{ students} \end{array}$$

There are 85 students in all who received free admission.

Step 4: Check your work. Estimate to see if the answer is reasonable. Round to the nearest ten, then add.

$$\begin{array}{r} 26 \\ 31 \\ +\ 28 \\ \hline 85 \end{array} \qquad \begin{array}{r} 30 \\ 30 \\ +\ 30 \\ \hline 90 \end{array}$$

85 is close to 90, so the answer is reasonable.

Addition Words

If you see one of these words or phrases, the word problem may be solved with addition.

add	additional	all	all together
and	both	combined	gain
greater	in all	more than	plus
raise	sum	together	total

Word Problem Power: Subtraction

Some word problems
compare numbers to find a difference.
Others separate a group into smaller groups.
Others start with an amount, then take some away.
All of these problems can be solved using subtraction.

Problem-Solving Strategies

Here are a few plans you can use to understand and solve problems.

Act It Out	**Make a Graph**	**Use Logical Reasoning**
Combine Strategies	**Make a Model**	**Work Backward**
Draw a Picture	**Make a Table**	**Write an Equation**
Find a Pattern	**Organize a List**	**Make Up Your Own!**
Guess, then Check	**Use Easier Numbers**	

Subtraction Word Problem

On Friday and Saturday night, Highland High School presented a musical comedy. In all, 1,623 people attended. On Saturday, 716 people attended. How many people came on Friday night?

Step 1: Read the problem. What do you know?
There were 1,623 people who saw the show. It ran on two nights. There were 716 people who came on Saturday.
What are you trying to find?
The number of people who came on Friday.

Step 2: Make a plan. The problem has a total for two nights, and separates the nightly attendance. This is a subtraction problem.
Start with the total, then subtract the number who came on Saturday to find the number who came on Friday.

Step 3: Follow the plan. Subtract the number on Saturday (716) from the total for both nights (1,623). Write the problem in a column, then subtract from right to left.

$$\begin{array}{r} 1\ \overset{1}{}\overset{13}{} \\ 16\overset{1}{2}\overset{13}{3} \\ -\ \ 716 \\ \hline 907 \end{array}$$

There were 907 people at the musical on Friday night.

Step 4: Check your work. Use addition to check subtraction.

$$\begin{array}{r} 1 \\ 907 \\ +\ 716 \\ \hline 1623 \end{array}$$

The sum is the same as the total for both nights, so the subtraction is correct.

Subtraction Words

If you see one of these words or phrases, the word problem may be solved with subtraction.

change	compare	decrease	difference
fewer	higher	larger	left
less than	longer	lost	minus
reduced	remain	subtract	take away

⑰ Adding Time

How many minutes do you spend
talking on the phone? How many hours?
How many hours do you spend on homework
each day? How many hours each week?

Adding Time

Add 2 hours 10 minutes + 4 hours 23 minutes.

To add time units, only
add units that are the same.
Hours only add to hours,
and minutes only
add to minutes.

Step 1: Write the problem in
columns. Line up units that
are the same.

```
  2 hours 10 minutes
+ 4 hours 23 minutes
```

Step 2: Add minutes.

```
  2 hours 10 minutes
+ 4 hours 23 minutes
          33 minutes
```

Step 3: Add hours.

```
  2 hours 10 minutes
+ 4 hours 23 minutes
  6 hours 33 minutes
```

2 hours 10 minutes + 4 hours 23 minutes = 6 hours 33 minutes

All types of measurement,
including time,
can be added, as long as you only
add units that are the same.

Units of Time

The list below shows the relationship between different units of time:

60 seconds = 1 minute	60 minutes = 1 hour
24 hours = 1 day	7 days = 1 week
52 weeks = 1 year	12 months = 1 year
365 days = 1 year	10 years = 1 decade
100 years = 1 century	1,000 years = 1 millennium

Regrouping Time

Add 6 hours 31 minutes + 2 hours 47 minutes.

Time values can be regrouped into other units. 60 minutes can be regrouped as 1 hour.

Step 1: Write the problem in columns. Line up units that are the same.

$$\begin{array}{r} 6 \text{ hours } 31 \text{ minutes} \\ + \ 2 \text{ hours } 47 \text{ minutes} \\ \hline \end{array}$$

Step 2: Add minutes. Do not write the sum in the answer until you regroup.

$$\begin{array}{r} 6 \text{ hours } 31 \text{ minutes} \\ + \ 2 \text{ hours } 47 \text{ minutes} \\ \hline 78 \text{ minutes} \end{array}$$

Step 3: Regroup minutes to hours.

78 minutes = 60 minutes + 18 minutes
= 1 hour + 18 minutes

Step 4: Write the regrouped hours and minutes.

$$\begin{array}{r} 1 \quad\quad\quad\quad\quad \\ 6 \text{ hours } 31 \text{ minutes} \\ + \ 2 \text{ hours } 47 \text{ minutes} \\ \hline 18 \text{ minutes} \end{array}$$

Step 5: Add hours.

$$\begin{array}{r} 1 \quad\quad\quad\quad\quad \\ 6 \text{ hours } 31 \text{ minutes} \\ + \ 2 \text{ hours } 47 \text{ minutes} \\ \hline 9 \text{ hours } 18 \text{ minutes} \end{array}$$

6 hours 31 minutes + 2 hours 47 minutes = 9 hours 18 minutes.

18 Subtracting Time

Units of time are subtracted like whole numbers. To regroup time units, you need to know how they relate to other time units. For example, one minute is the same as 60 seconds.

Subtracting Time

Dean ran a race in 7 minutes 12 seconds. Andre ran the race in 5 minutes 51 seconds. How much faster than Dean did Andre run?

Subtract Andre's time from Dean's time to find how much faster Andre ran one mile.

Step 1: Write the problem in columns. Line up units that are the same.

$$\begin{array}{r} 7 \text{ minutes } 12 \text{ seconds} \\ - \ 5 \text{ minutes } 51 \text{ seconds} \end{array}$$

Step 2: There are not enough seconds to subtract. Regroup 7 minutes as 6 minutes and 60 seconds. Add 60 seconds to the seconds column. 60 + 12 = 72

$$\begin{array}{r} 6 \qquad\quad 72 \\ \not{7} \text{ minutes } \not{12} \text{ seconds} \\ - \ 5 \text{ minutes } 51 \text{ seconds} \end{array}$$

Step 3: Subtract seconds. 72 – 51 = 21

$$\begin{array}{r} 6 \qquad\quad 72 \\ \not{7} \text{ minutes } \not{12} \text{ seconds} \\ - \ 5 \text{ minutes } 51 \text{ seconds} \\ \hline 21 \text{ seconds} \end{array}$$

Step 4: Subtract minutes. 6 – 5 = 1

$$\begin{array}{r} 6 \qquad\quad 72 \\ \not{7} \text{ minutes } \not{12} \text{ seconds} \\ - \ 5 \text{ minutes } 51 \text{ seconds} \\ \hline 1 \text{ minute } \ 21 \text{ seconds} \end{array}$$

Andre ran the race 1 minute and 21 seconds faster than Dean.

Elapsed Time

Time that has passed is called elapsed time. It is the difference in time from when something begins to when it ends.

At 7:30 A.M., you left your house. It is now 3:45 P.M. How much time has elapsed since you left your house this morning?

One of the easiest ways to find elapsed time is to count on from the beginning time to the ending time.

Step 1: Count the number of whole hours first.

      7:30, 8:30, 9:30, 10:30, 11:30, 12:30, 1:30, 2:30, 3:30
        1h   2h   3h   4h   5h   6h   7h   8h

There are 8 full hours from 7:30 A.M. to 3:30 P.M.

Step 2: Count the number of minutes from 3:30 P.M. to 3:45 P.M. You may count in 5-minute intervals.

      3:30,   3:35,   3:40,   3:45
             5 min   10 min   15 min

There are 15 minutes from 3:30 P.M. to 3:45 P.M.

Step 3: Combine the hours and minutes.   **8 hours + 15 minutes**

From the time you left your house this morning, 8 hours 15 minutes have elapsed.

12-Hour and 24-Hour Time

A clock helps measure the time in a 24-hour day.
A day begins at midnight and ends at the next midnight.

12-hour time: Most clocks show twelve hours, and go around twice in a day.
The 12 hours from midnight until noon are labeled A.M.
The 12 hours from noon until midnight are labeled P.M.

24-hour time: A 24-hour clock begins at midnight and end the following midnight. The hours after noon in 24-hour time are 12 more than they are in 12-hour time.
For example, 1:30 P.M. is 13:30 in 24-hour time.

⑲ Adding Decimals

Decimal numbers show
values that are not whole numbers.
They are also used every day in measurements,
in sports statistics, and to represent money.

Decimal Place Value

Digits to the left of the decimal point are whole numbers.
Digits to the right of the decimal point are part of a whole number.

	34.56			
tens	ones	.	tenths	hundredths
3	4	.	5	6
3 tens	4 ones	.	5 tenths	6 hundredths

Adding Decimals

Add 5.2 + 1.4

Any decimals can be added.
Line up the decimal points, then add.

Step 1: Write the numbers in a column.
Line up decimal points. When the decimal
points are lined up, all of the places
are also lined up.

$$\begin{array}{r} 5.2 \\ + \ 1.4 \\ \hline \end{array}$$

Step 2: Add each place, beginning
on the right. Add tenths. 2 + 4 = 6
Write the decimal point in the answer.

$$\begin{array}{r} 5.2 \\ + \ 1.4 \\ \hline .6 \end{array}$$

Step 3: Add ones. 5 + 1 = 6

5.2 + 1.4 = 6.6

$$\begin{array}{r} 5.2 \\ + \ 1.4 \\ \hline 6.6 \end{array}$$

Uneven Digits

*One month there were
2.63 inches of rain.
The following month there
were 4.5 inches inches of rain.
How many inches of rain
were there in all?*

Step 1: Write the numbers in a column.
Line up decimal points.

$$\begin{array}{r} 2.63 \\ +\ 4.5\ \\ \hline \end{array}$$

Step 2: One of the numbers ends in the
hundreths place. The other ends in the tenths.
To make it easier to add, you can put zeros on
the right side of a decimal without changing the value.

$$\begin{array}{r} 2.63 \\ +\ 4.50 \\ \hline \end{array}$$

Step 3: Add hundredths.

$$\begin{array}{r} 2.63 \\ +\ 4.50 \\ \hline 3 \end{array}$$

Step 4: Add tenths.

$$\begin{array}{r} 1 \\ 2.63 \\ +\ 4.50 \\ \hline .13 \end{array}$$

Step 5: Add ones.

$$\begin{array}{r} 1 \\ 2.63 \\ +\ 4.50 \\ \hline 7.13 \end{array}$$

**There were 7.13 inches
of rain in all.**

You can add
zeros to the right side
of a decimal without
changing the value.

$1.2 = 1.20 = 1.200 = 1.2000$

⑳ Subtracting Decimals

When you know how to subtract whole numbers, you also know how to subtract decimals. Adding and subtracting decimals uses place value, just like adding and subtracting whole numbers.

Decimal Subtraction

Here are a few things to remember when you subtract decimals:

- Line up the decimal points. The place values will line up when the decimal points are lined up.
- Use zeros as place holders in empty places at the end of decimals. They don't change the value.
- Subtract from right to left.
- Regroup whenever you need to. Regrouping decimals is done the same way as regrouping whole numbers.

Subtracting Decimals

Subtract 6.2 – 2.

Step 1: Line up decimal points.
In a whole number, the decimal point is at the end.
Write a zero as a place holder after
the decimal point in the whole number 2.

$$\begin{array}{r} 6.2 \\ -\ 2.0 \\ \hline \end{array}$$

Step 2: Subtract tenths.
Write the decimal point in the answer.

$$\begin{array}{r} 6.2 \\ -\ 2.0 \\ \hline .2 \end{array}$$

Step 3: Subtract ones.

6.2 – 2 = 4.2

$$\begin{array}{r} 6.2 \\ -\ 2.0 \\ \hline 4.2 \end{array}$$

Regrouping Decimals

Subtract 16.8 from 124.2.

Some problems are written without the minus sign (–).
Read the problem carefully before you try to solve it.

Step 1: Write the numbers in a column.
Line up decimal points.

$$
\begin{array}{r}
124.2 \\
-\ \ 16.8 \\
\hline
\end{array}
$$

Step 2: Regroup 1 one as 10 tenths.
Subtract tenths.

$$
\begin{array}{r}
3\ 12 \\
12\cancel{4}.2 \\
-\ \ 16.8 \\
\hline
.4
\end{array}
$$

Step 3: Regroup 1 ten as 10 ones.
Subtract ones.

$$
\begin{array}{r}
13 \\
1\ \cancel{3}\ 12 \\
12\cancel{4}.2 \\
-\ \ 16.8 \\
\hline
7.4
\end{array}
$$

Step 4: Subtract tens.

$$
\begin{array}{r}
13 \\
1\ \cancel{3}\ 12 \\
12\cancel{4}.2 \\
-\ \ 16.8 \\
\hline
07.4
\end{array}
$$

Step 5: Subtract hundreds.

124.2 – 16.8 = 107.4

$$
\begin{array}{r}
13 \\
1\ \cancel{3}\ 12 \\
12\cancel{4}.2 \\
-\ \ 16.8 \\
\hline
107.4
\end{array}
$$

Decimals are numbers that use a decimal point to separate whole number values from values that are less than a whole.

21 Adding Money

Money values are written as decimal numbers. You add money just like decimals.

Value in Dollars

This table shows the value of coins and bills written as decimals.

Coin	Value in Dollars	Bill	Value in Dollars
1 penny	$0.01	one-dollar	$1.00
1 nickel	$0.05	five-dollar	$5.00
1 dime	$0.10	ten-dollar	$10.00
1 quarter	$0.25	twenty-dollar	$20.00
1 half-dollar	$0.50	fifty-dollar	$50.00
1 dollar	$1.00	one-hundred-dollar	$100.00

Adding Decimals

Thom has a ten-dollar bill, 2 quarters, 1 nickel, and 3 pennies. Jenny has a five-dollar bill, 1 quarter, and 2 dimes. How much money do they have in all?

Money amounts that are written as decimals are added like any other decimal. Begin adding in the hundreths place.

Step 1: Find how much Thom has. First, change each piece of money into its decimal value.

1 ten-dollar bill	2 quarters	1 nickel	3 pennies
$10.00	$0.25	$0.05	$0.01
	+ $0.25		$0.01
	$0.50		+ $0.01
			$0.03

Step 2: Add to find Thom's total.

$10.00
$ 0.50
$ 0.05
+ $ 0.03
$10.58

Step 3: In the same way, find how much money Jenny has.

1 five-dollar bill	1 quarter	2 dimes
$5.00	$0.25	$0.10
		+ $0.10
		$0.20

Step 4: Add to find Jenny's total.

$5.00
$0.25
+ $0.20
$5.45

Step 5: Thom has $10.58. Jenny has $5.45. Add to find how much they have in all.

| |
$10.58
+ $ 5.45
$16.03

In all, Thom and Jenny have $16.03.

Remember to line up the decimal points when adding decimals.

When adding dollar amounts, be sure to write a decimal point and the dollar sign in the answer.

47

Subtracting Money

Subtracting money values
is the same as subtracting decimal values.

Subtracting Money

Matilda got a $500.00 MediaMart gift card for her birthday. She spent $347.68 using the card. How much more can she spend using the card?

To solve this problem, subtract $500.00 − $347.68.

Step 1: Write the numbers in a column. Line up decimal points.

$$\begin{array}{r} \$500.00 \\ -\ \$347.68 \\ \hline \end{array}$$

Step 2: You must regroup before you can subtract. There are no tenths, ones, or tens to regroup. Regroup 1 hundred as 10 tens. Regroup 1 ten as 10 ones. Regroup 1 one as 10 tenths. Regroup 1 tenth as 10 hundredths.

$$\begin{array}{r} 9\ \ 9\ \ 9 \\ 4\ 10\ 10\ 10\ 10 \\ \$500.00 \\ -\ \$347.68 \\ \hline \end{array}$$

Step 3: Subtract from right to left.

Matilda has $152.32 left to spend on her gift card.

$$\begin{array}{r} 9\ \ 9\ \ 9 \\ 4\ 10\ 10\ 10\ 10 \\ \$500.00 \\ -\ \$347.68 \\ \hline \$152.32 \end{array}$$

Fact Buster!

Solve money problems by knowing how to add and subtract decimals!

Reading Money Values

When you read a money value, you read in dollars and cents.

$15.62

The digits on the left of the decimal point are whole dollar amounts. Read the whole number, then say "dollars."

The digits on the right of the decimal point are fractions of a dollar, in hundredths. They are read as cents. Read the two-digit number, then say "cents."

Fifteen dollars sixty-two cents

When you read a decimal, you say "and" for the decimal point. In a money value, you can say "and," but it is not necessary.

Fifteen dollars and sixty-two cents

Making Change

How much change should you get if you spend $3.74, and you give the clerk $5.00?

Finding the amount of change is a subtraction problem. An easy way to make change is to begin at the cost, then count up using coins and bills.

Step 1: Use coins to count up from $3.74 to the next dollar amount.

$3.74
A penny ($0.01) more is $3.75.
A quarter ($0.25) more is $4.00.

A penny and a quarter are $0.26.

Step 2: Count up with bills to reach $5.00.

$4.00
One-dollar bill ($1.00) more is $5.00.

You should get a $1-bill, a quarter, and a penny, which is a total of $1.26 in change.

Integers are simply all positive
whole numbers, their opposites, and 0.
2 is a whole number. 2 is positive.
⁻2 is the opposite of 2. ⁻2 is negative.
Zero is a neutral integer. It is not positive or negative.

$$-5 \;\; -4 \;\; -3 \;\; -2 \;\; -1 \;\; 0 \;\; 1 \;\; 2 \;\; 3 \;\; 4 \;\; 5$$

Opposites

Positive numbers are
usually written without
the positive sign. The
integer ⁺4 has the same
meaning as 4.

Adding Like Integers

Integers that have the same sign
are called like integers.

Add ⁻4 + ⁻2.

Step 1: To add like integers, pretend the signs are not there.	⁻4 + ⁻2 ⁺4 + ⁺2
Step 2: Add the numbers.	4 + 2 = 6
Step 3: Put the same sign as the addends on the sum.	⁻4 + ⁻2 = ⁻6

Add ⁺7 + ⁺9.

Step 1: Pretend the signs are not there.	⁺7 + ⁺9 ⁺7 + ⁺9
Step 2: Add the numbers.	7 + 9 = 16
Step 3: Put the same sign as the addends on the sum.	⁺7 + ⁺9 = ⁺16, or 16

Adding Unlike Integers

One positive unit and one negative unit cancel each other out.

That means when you add 1 + ⁻1, the sum is 0.

Add ⁻ 3 + 5.

Step 1: Imagine each negative unit is a red circle, and each positive unit is a blue circle.

Step 2: One negative cancels out one positive. Three negatives cancel out three positives. There are 2 blue (positive) circles left.

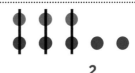

2

⁻3 + 5 = 2

You can use subtraction to add unlike integers.

Add 8 + ⁻ 10.

Step 1: Pretend the signs are not there.

$$8 + {}^-10$$
$$8 \quad {}^{\prime}10$$

Step 2: Subtract the smaller number (8) from the larger number (10).

$$10 - 8 = 2$$

Step 3: Give the answer the same sign as the larger number. The larger number is 10. The 10 has a negative sign. Give the answer a negative sign.

⁻2

8 + ⁻10 = ⁻2

Addition Rules for Unlike Integers:

When the larger number is positive, the answer is positive.

When the larger number is negative, the answer is negative.

㉔ Subtracting Integers

Integers are subtracted by
adding the opposite.

Subtracting Integers

*On Monday the temperature
was 5° Fahrenheit.
On Tuesday the temperature
was ⁻3° Fahrenheit.
What was the difference in
temperature between
Monday and Tuesday?*

To solve this problem, subtract 5 – ⁻3.

Step 1: Instead of subtracting, add the opposite.   5 – ⁻3
Change the subtraction sign to an addition sign.   5 + 3
Change the integer being subtracted to
its opposite (⁻3 becomes 3).

Step 2: The signs are the same. Pretend the   5 + 3 = 8
signs aren't there. Add the numbers.
Put the sign from the addends on the sum.

5 – ⁻3 = 8. The difference in temperature was 8° Fahrenheit.

Negative numbers
are often used in
science and accounting.

Amounts you owe,
temperatures below zero,
and elevations below sea level are
all written as negative numbers.

Subtract ⁻11 – ⁻2.

| **Step 1:** Instead of subtracting, add the opposite. | ⁻11 – ⁻2 |
| Rewrite the subtraction as addition. | ⁻11 + 2 |

Step 2: The signs are different.   ⁻11 + 2   ⁻11   2
Pretend the signs are not there.
Subtract the smaller number from the larger number.   11 – 2 = 9
The larger number (11) is negative,
so the answer is negative.   ⁻11 + 2 = ⁻9

⁻11 – ⁻2 = ⁻9

Subtract 7 – 19.

| **Step 1:** Instead of subtracting, add the opposite. | 7 – 19 |
| Rewrite the subtraction as addition. | 7 + ⁻19 |

Step 2: The signs are different.   7 + ⁻19   7   ⁻19
Pretend the signs are not there.
Subtract the smaller number from the larger number. 19 – 7 = 12
The larger number (19) is negative,
so the answer is negative.   7 + ⁻19 = ⁻12

7 – 19 = ⁻12

Integer Addition and Subtraction Rules

Adding integers with the same sign:
Pretend the signs are not there. Add the numbers. Put the sign from the addends on the sum.

Adding integers with different signs:
Pretend the signs are not there. Find the difference. Put the sign of the larger addend on the sum.

Subtracting integers:
Add the opposite integer. Follow the integer addition rules.

25 Adding **Fractions**

A fraction is a number
that stands for part of a whole unit,
or part of a set.

Fractions

Here are some fraction terms you should know.

denominator—The bottom number in a fraction.
It tells the total number of equal parts.

numerator—The top number in a fraction.
It tells the number of parts being talked about.

like fractions—Fractions that have the same, or common, denominator. $\frac{1}{5}$ and $\frac{3}{5}$ are like fractions.

unlike fractions—Fractions that have different denominators. $\frac{1}{4}$ and $\frac{3}{7}$ are unlike fractions.

Adding Like Fractions

Add $\frac{3}{6} + \frac{2}{6}$.

Step 1: To add like fractions,
add only the numerators.

$$\frac{3}{6} + \frac{2}{6} = \frac{3+2}{6} = \frac{5}{6}$$

Step 2: Keep the same denominator.

$$\frac{3}{6} + \frac{2}{6} = \frac{5}{6}$$

$$\frac{3}{6} + \frac{2}{6} = \frac{5}{6}$$

Adding Unlike Fractions

Add $\frac{1}{4} + \frac{3}{8}$.

Step 1: Look at the denominators. They are different. Before you can add these fractions, you need to make the denominators the same.

$$\frac{1}{4} \quad \frac{3}{8}$$

Step 2: Give $\frac{1}{4}$ a denominator of 8 by multiplying the numerator and denominator each by 2.

$$\frac{1}{4} = \frac{1 \times 2}{4 \times 2} = \frac{2}{8}$$

Step 3: Write the problem using like fractions.

$$\frac{1}{4} + \frac{3}{8}$$

is the same as $\frac{2}{8} + \frac{3}{8}$

Step 4: Add the numerators. Keep the common denominator.

$$\frac{2}{8} + \frac{3}{8} = \frac{2 + 3}{8} = \frac{5}{8}$$

$$\frac{1}{4} + \frac{3}{8} = \frac{5}{8}$$

Add $\frac{1}{12} + \frac{1}{3}$.

Step 1: Give the fractions a common denominator.

$$\frac{1}{3} = \frac{1 \times 4}{3 \times 4} = \frac{4}{12}$$

Step 2: Rewrite the problem.

$\frac{1}{12} + \frac{1}{3}$ is the same as $\frac{1}{12} + \frac{4}{12}$

Step 3: Add the numerators. Keep the common denominator.

$$\frac{1}{12} + \frac{4}{12} = \frac{1 + 4}{12} = \frac{5}{12}$$

$$\frac{1}{12} + \frac{1}{3} = \frac{5}{12}$$

Multiplying or dividing the numerator and denominator by the same number does not change the value of a fraction. Fractions with the same value are called **equivalent fractions**.

$$\frac{1}{2} = \frac{1 \times 2}{2 \times 2} = \frac{2}{4} \qquad \frac{3}{6} = \frac{3 \div 3}{6 \div 3} = \frac{1}{2}$$

55

26 Subtracting **Fractions**

When you add fractions,
you add only the numerators,
and keep the common denominator.
Subtracting fractions is done in the same way.

Subtracting Like Fractions

*Permission slips for a museum trip were
given out on Friday. Only 4 out of 9
students, or $\frac{4}{9}$, returned the form on
Monday. One of the returned
forms, or $\frac{1}{9}$, was not signed.
What fraction of the students
returned signed forms on Monday?*

To solve this problem, subtract $\frac{4}{9} - \frac{1}{9}$.

Step 1: To subtract like fractions,
subtract only the numerators.
Keep the common denominator.

$$\frac{4}{9} - \frac{1}{9} = \frac{4-1}{9} = \frac{3}{9}$$

Step 2: Reduce the answer to lowest terms.
To do this, find the factors of the numerator and denominator.

Factors of 3: 1, **3**
Factors of 9: 1, **3**, 9
The greatest factor they have in common is 3.

Divide the numerator and denominator by the
greatest common factor, 3.

$$\frac{3}{9} = \frac{3 \div 3}{9 \div 3} = \frac{1}{3}$$

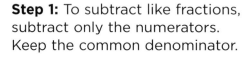

$$\frac{4}{9} - \frac{1}{9} = \frac{1}{3}$$

$\frac{1}{3}$ **of the students returned signed permission forms on Monday.**

Factors and Multiples

Knowing about factors and multiples will help you find common denominators, and write fractions in lowest terms.

common factor—A number that divides evenly into two or more numbers. The number 2 divides evenly into 8 and 10. The number 2 is a common factor of 8 and 10.

greatest common factor—The largest number that divides evenly into two or more numbers.

multiple—The product of a number and any whole number is a multiple of that number. Some multiples of 2 are 2, 4, 6, and 8.

common multiple—A number that is a multiple of two or more numbers.

least common multiple—The smallest common multiple, other than zero, of two or more numbers.

Subtracting Unlike Fractions

Subtract $\frac{1}{2} - \frac{3}{8}$.

Step 1: Make the denominators the same. To do this, look at the multiples of the two denominators.

Multiples of 2 are 2, 4, 6, **8**, 10, . . .
Multiples of 8 are **8**, 16, 24, . . .   The least common multiple is 8.

Write a fraction for $\frac{1}{2}$ that has a denominator of 8.

$$\frac{1}{2} = \frac{1 \times 4}{2 \times 4} = \frac{4}{8}$$

Step 2: Write the problem using like fractions.

$$\frac{4}{8} - \frac{3}{8}$$

Step 3: Subtract.

$$\frac{4}{8} - \frac{3}{8} = \frac{4 - 3}{8} = \frac{1}{8}$$

$$\frac{1}{2} - \frac{3}{8} = \frac{1}{8}$$

Mixed numbers have two parts,
a whole number and a fraction. It is a mix.

Adding Mixed Numbers

*Mitchell ate $2\frac{1}{4}$ cups of cereal for breakfast. Then he
ate $1\frac{1}{2}$ cups more as a late-night snack.*

How many cups of cereal did Mitchell eat in all?

To solve this problem, add $2\frac{1}{4}$ + $1\frac{1}{2}$.

Step 1: Add the fraction part.
Find a common denominator, then add.

$$\frac{1}{4} + \frac{1}{2}$$

$$\frac{1}{4} + \frac{2}{4}$$

$$\frac{1}{4} + \frac{2}{4} = \frac{1+2}{4} = \frac{3}{4}$$

Step 2: Add the whole numbers. $2 + 1 = 3$

Step 3: Put the sum of the whole numbers
and the sum of the fractions together.

Sum of whole numbers: **3**

Sum of fractions: $\frac{3}{4}$

Mixed number: $3\frac{3}{4}$

$$2\frac{1}{4} + 1\frac{1}{2} = 3\frac{3}{4}$$

Mitchell ate $3\frac{3}{4}$ cups of cereal in all.

Regrouping Mixed Numbers

In mixed number addition, the sum of the fractions might be an improper fraction. This means the numerator is equal to or greater than the denominator.

Kara ran $2\frac{2}{3}$ miles. Clay ran $2\frac{1}{3}$ miles. How many miles did Kara and Clay run combined?

To solve this problem, add $2\frac{2}{3} + 2\frac{1}{3}$.

Step 1: Add the fraction parts.

$$\begin{array}{r} 2\frac{2}{3} \\ + 2\frac{1}{3} \\ \hline \frac{3}{3} \end{array}$$

Step 2: Regroup the fraction sum and carry to the whole numbers. When the numerator and denominator are the same, the value is 1.

$$\begin{array}{r} ^{1}2\frac{2}{3} \\ + 2\frac{1}{3} \\ \hline \frac{\cancel{3}}{\cancel{3}} \end{array}$$

Step 3: Add the whole numbers.
1 + 2 + 2 = 5

$2\frac{2}{3} + 2\frac{1}{3} = 5$

Kara and Clay ran 5 miles combined.

$$\begin{array}{r} ^{1}2\frac{2}{3} \\ + 2\frac{1}{3} \\ \hline 5 \end{array}$$

Improper fractions are fractions with a numerator that is equal to or greater than the denominator.

Mixed numbers can be subtracted in more than one way.

Subtracting Mixed Numbers

Sydney is making a batch of cookies that calls for $3\frac{1}{3}$ cups of flour. She has $1\frac{2}{3}$ cups of flour left in a container. How many more cups of flour does she need?

Subtract $3\frac{1}{3} - 1\frac{2}{3}$ to find how many more cups of flour she needs.

Step 1: $\frac{2}{3}$ is bigger than $\frac{1}{3}$ so regroup 1 whole as $\frac{3}{3}$.

$$3\frac{1}{3} = 2 + \frac{3}{3} + \frac{1}{3} = 2\frac{4}{3}$$
$$-\ 1\frac{2}{3} \qquad\qquad\qquad -\ 1\frac{2}{3}$$

Step 2: Subtract the fractions.

$$2\frac{4}{3}$$
$$-\ 1\frac{2}{3}$$
$$\overline{\frac{2}{3}}$$

Step 3: Subtract the whole numbers.

$$2\frac{4}{3}$$
$$-\ 1\frac{2}{3}$$
$$\overline{1\frac{2}{3}}$$

Sydney still needs $1\frac{2}{3}$ cups of flour.

Subtracting Improper Fractions

Subtract $2\frac{1}{8} - 1\frac{1}{4}$.

Step 1: Rename the mixed numbers as improper fractions.

One way to do this is to multiply the denominator by the whole number, then add the numerator. This becomes the numerator. The denominator stays the same.

$$2\frac{1}{8} = \frac{(8 \times 2) + 1}{8} = \frac{17}{8}$$

Another way is to regroup the whole number as a fraction with the same denominator. Add the two parts.

$$1\frac{1}{4} = \frac{4}{4} + \frac{1}{4} = \frac{5}{4}$$

Step 2: Use equivalent fractions to give them a common denominator.

$$\frac{5}{4} = \frac{5 \times 2}{4 \times 2} = \frac{10}{8}$$

Step 3: Rewrite the problem with improper fractions and common denominators.

$$2\frac{1}{8} - 1\frac{1}{4} = \frac{17}{8} - \frac{10}{8}$$

Step 4: Subtract.

$$\frac{17}{8} - \frac{10}{8} = \frac{17 - 10}{8} = \frac{7}{8}$$

$$2\frac{1}{8} - 1\frac{1}{4} = \frac{7}{8}$$

Fractions that have a numerator and denominator that are the same are equal to 1.

$$1 = \frac{4}{4} = \frac{2}{2} = \frac{12}{12} = \frac{3}{3}$$

Whole numbers can be written as improper fractions by putting the number over a 1.

$$2 = \frac{2}{1} \qquad 5 = \frac{5}{1}$$

Further Reading

Books

Great Source Education Group, Inc. *Math At Hand.* Wilmington, Mass.:
    Great Source Education Group, Inc., 2006.

Fisher, Richard W. *Mastering Essential Math Skills.* Los Gatos, Calif.:
    Math Essentials, 2001.

Internet Addresses

A+ Math. "Aplusmath.com Worksheets." © 1998–2007.
    <http://www.aplusmath.com/Worksheets/index.html>

Dositey Corporation. "Math." © 1998–2005.
    <http://www.dositey.com/math58.htm>

The Math Forum. "Ask Dr. Math" © 1994–2007.
    <http://mathforum.org/library/drmath/sets/elem_addition.html>
    <http://mathforum.org/library/drmath/sets/elem_subtraction.html>

Index